FOOTBALL
LEGENDS

GARETH SOUTHGATE

ED HAWKINS

FOOTBALL LEGENDS

GARETH SOUTHGATE

SCHOLASTIC

Published in the UK by Scholastic, 2022
1 London Bridge, London SE1 9BA
Scholastic Ireland, 89E Lagan Road, Dublin Industrial Estate,
Glasnevin, Dublin, D11 HP5F

Text © Ed Hawkins, 2022
Cover illustration © Stanley Chow, 2022

ISBN 978 07023 1701 9

A CIP catalogue record for this book is available from the British Library.

Printed and bound by CPI Group (UK) Ltd, Croydon, CR0 4YY
Paper made from wood grown in sustainable forests and other
controlled sources.

3 5 7 9 10 8 6 4

www.scholastic.co.uk

Contents

While this book is based on real people and actual events, some situations and conversations are fictional, created by the author.

MAKING OF A HERO

Heroes can come in all shapes and sizes. Gareth Southgate is proof of that.

As a boy no one who saw him walking down the street would have believed he would play football professionally at the highest level for club and country. He was slightly awkward looking.

But he had lots of guts and determination to make it in one of the toughest sports in the world. He had an early start. His first lesson in the rough and tumble of football came at the age of three when he chased a ball at home, ran into a glass door and cut his head open.

As a player, he didn't come across as the sort who would, one day, take a failing football nation and, calmly, quietly, make them one of the most feared teams on the planet.

Gareth, as you will find out, was "too nice". Football managers are supposed to be shouters and screamers. They are supposed to bully people until they get what they want. But Gareth was nothing like that.

In fact though, he would be the perfect fit for a national team which had become a laughing stock. England, would you believe, were so bad at international football that when a World Cup or a European Championship approached, the country was not that interested.

Not any more. Gareth played a huge part in changing all that.

Born in Watford on 3 September 1970, Gareth became a star athlete and footballer at primary and secondary school. He played professionally for Crystal Palace before moving on to Aston Villa, then Middlesbrough. He won championships and trophies.

He played for England, scored for England,

captained England. Yet as a player he was remembered most for missing a penalty in the European Championships in 1996, costing the team a place in the final. That was what he was famous for. It was one of the reasons why English football had become a joke. This story is about how he changed that.

IN THE BEGINNING

Once he got over that cut on his head, Gareth played football as often as he could and for as long as he could. All day and every day, if he was allowed!

As he got older, he was the best player for Pound Hill Primary School in Crawley, England. Sometimes his team won and sometimes they didn't. When they lost, Gareth would find a seat by himself at the back of the team minibus and cry. He was embarrassed and didn't want his teammates to notice. But they noticed in the end.

Gareth couldn't stand losing. Once his mum had joked, "If you lose, you won't get any dinner."

His school friends would laugh, "No wonder he's crying – he's not going to get anything to eat!" It didn't matter what the sport was, if Gareth's team lost, he'd cry. And he was teased for it.

Home Life

The young Gareth was always on the move. His dad's job meant that they had to move round the country a lot. He worked for IBM, the computer company. The Southgates lived in Bury, Portsmouth and, finally, Crawley, in Sussex.

His dad, Clive, had wanted to be a professional footballer, too. He signed for Luton Town Football Club as a schoolboy. But despite his passion for games and sport – he was also good at athletics and rugby union – he knew that his chances of making a decent living in sport were small.

Clive met Gareth's mum, Barbara, when they were both competing for Hertfordshire in the English Schools' athletics meeting. Clive was a javelin thrower. Barbara was competing in the hurdles.

Clive was quiet and Gareth never saw him lose his temper. Clive didn't get excited watching Gareth play football, either. He didn't shout and encourage from the touchline, like most of the other parents. And if Gareth got injured, he would just ask quietly, "Are you okay?"

Clive was Gareth's hero. He was determined that when he grew up, he would be just like his dad; calm, thoughtful and putting his family first. Clive had been brought up by his aunt and grandmother after his mum had died when he was a baby. His dad had been reported killed in the Second World War. But in fact, Clive's dad had met another woman and emigrated to Canada.

THE FOOTBALL LIFE

Gareth always knew he was going to be a footballer, although he could have been anything he wanted – his schoolwork was excellent. University would have been a breeze, but that never entered his head. "Football will be my life," he decided. "And one day, I might even get to play for England."

Just what was it about Gareth that made him a future England player? Well, not surprisingly, Gareth was usually the best player on the pitch. If he wanted to, he could dribble from one end of the pitch to the other, beating everyone before scoring. But Gareth was different. Despite being able to do that, he rarely did. Instead, he would beat a few players and then play the killer ball for someone else to score. What really made him stand out was that he was an unselfish team player. Even at a young age, he had an understanding, or reading, of the game like few others.

During his second year at Pound Hill Primary School he would go to watch the matches and all the older boys wanted him in the school team. Mr Cripps, the football coach, said he had to wait his turn. At the age of nine, he played in his local team, Crawley Traders Under-12s. His dad coached the team and in winter, they had to train in a multi-storey car park because it had lights and the training pitch didn't.

His dad would be willing him on from the touchline in his own quiet way. Instead of being a dad who would cheer and shout, "Go on, son!" Clive would instead discuss Gareth's performance with him in the car on the way home or over their evening meal.

If Gareth thought that there'd been an opposition player who was better than him, his dad would reassure him, "Don't worry, you're the better player."

But he wouldn't lie about Gareth's ability. If there was someone who did have a superior skill, he would admit, "Yes, he's better in the air than you." This made Gareth aware of the improvements he needed to make in his game.

If his dad was unable to make it to a match because of work, Gareth would relive every kick, header and tackle over the dinner table – what he did right and what he did wrong. And his dad would listen patiently.

Gareth's life was all about football – playing it whenever he could, then talking about it: how he played, how the opposition played and how his teammates played. And he loved to watch football, too: his favourite TV programme was *Match of the Day* and he was a devoted Manchester United fan.

MAKING HIS MARK

When he turned eleven, Gareth went to Hazelwick Comprehensive in Crawley. He made an immediate impression in the football trials for the school team.

"I saw quite a small boy just gliding around the pitches looking totally in control – of himself and of the ball," football coach Dave Palmer said. "We all just looked at each other and went: 'Wow!'"

Not surprisingly, sport was Gareth's favourite subject at school. He absolutely loved athletics. At primary school, the kids were too young to take part in proper, organized sessions. But at Hazelwick it was different. He was taught how to run; how to jump; how to be, well, athletic!

Gareth turned into a brilliant athlete. He became the county schools champion at triple jump and held the school record for years. He was also one of the best 200-metre runners in the area. Not content with athletics, Gareth also played basketball and rugby union, where he played at fly-half – the most creative job in the team.

At Hazelwick of course, the teachers still ask their pupils: "Did you know Gareth Southgate went to this school?" And the students' eyes go wide with amazement. The teachers tell them how that polite, fiercely determined and competitive young man not only shone at football – he could do it all.

They also tell the story of how the school under-14s football team went on tour to France and had to change in a barn before a game. They show the students a photo of thirteen-year-old Gareth, beaming excitedly, in the team's red-and-white striped shirt.

Pain

However, Gareth had to pay a horrible price for all that running, jumping, tackling and dribbling. He started to feel pain in his knees, and it got worse and worse. Every night he went to bed hoping that the pain would be better in the morning, that it would be gone.

But it didn't go away. It started to affect his football and other sports. Gareth went to the doctor, expecting to be told that he had suffered a small injury and would be fit again after a little rest. But no – instead he was diagnosed with a condition which could mean that his dreams of a professional career were over.

Gareth had Osgood–Schlatter disease, which affects growing adolescents and causes severe pain in the knees. It's a condition where the lower leg bone swells up and rubs against the knee joint, making it especially sore when you exercise.

The pain would only stop if Gareth stopped. And by stop, the doctor meant stop everything. So for four long months, Gareth was not allowed to play any sport whatsoever.

His dad remembers it making Gareth sad and angry. "It tore him apart," Clive says. Gareth felt like he was getting left behind, with his teammates getting fitter and more skilful while he had to stay at home with his feet up.

In his absence, Hazelwick made it to the final of the district cup competition. And, would you believe, Gareth's managerial career started early. Just because he couldn't play, that didn't mean he couldn't watch. From the touchline he relived every kick and header in those games he missed and gave out tactical advice and encouragement to his teammates.

"We got to the final, but Gareth couldn't play," David Palmer said. "He came to every single match and was supportive. He was like my assistant manager. We played the final at Crystal Palace's ground, so that would have been a big thing for him to miss. But he never showed it. He was a delight to work with, and so supportive of the other boys in the team, no matter how good they were."

SCOUTED

After four months of rest, Gareth's knees were much better and he was able to attend a football course in the summer holidays. While attending the course, the eleven-year-old Gareth was talent-scouted. A Southampton Football Club (FC) scout liked what he saw and picked Gareth out as one of the best players. Would he like to train with them at one of Southampton's centres of excellence? You bet he would!

Southampton FC had one of the best youth systems in England, with centres of excellence all around the country. Gareth would train on a Friday night and play against teams from the club's other centres. He especially remembers one strong and fast centre-forward who played for the Newcastle centre of excellence. It was Alan Shearer, his future England teammate.

But Gareth's time with Southampton FC would be his first harsh lesson of the football life. After two-and-a-half years, Southampton decided they didn't want to keep him. They said he was too small. Gareth was devastated, particularly as they told him by letter and didn't even get his dad's name right!

The letter read: "Dear Gareth Southgate, We will not be offering your son a place…" They thought his dad was called Gareth. It hurt him and to this day, he still has that letter. He kept it as a reminder that there would always be people who didn't think he would be good enough. And he also kept it because he didn't just want to be the boy "let go by Southampton". He wanted to prove them wrong.

Another chance

When playing for a district team in Crawley at thirteen, Gareth was spotted by an Arsenal scout,

Fred Ricketts. Fred saw that Gareth could play but was also worried that he wasn't big or strong enough. Fred spoke to Clive and told him to get his son playing in a stronger league. So Clive looked around for competitive action which would test his son physically, and settled on Seldon Juniors in the Shirley and District League in Croydon. There, Gareth quickly came to grips with the physical side of the game.

The coach at Seldon Juniors was Derek Millen, who also worked as a scout for league club Crystal Palace. When he noticed Gareth's potential, he quickly got on the phone to his Palace colleagues. Gareth was invited to train with the Crystal Palace youth team. The team was run by Alan Smith.

Within a few weeks Gareth was taken aside and told, "You're playing at Oxford on Saturday in the third team." Gareth was confused. The third team? He went home to look in a club programme to see if there were three youth sides.

There weren't. The team Gareth had been asked to play for was the South East Counties XI, which was the third *senior* team at the club, after the first team and the reserves. Gareth would be playing men's football at the age of just fifteen!

Gareth was a substitute for the match, which was played at Oxford United's crumbling Manor Ground. The pitch sloped dramatically from one end to the other. There were seven different stands. It looked nothing like a football stadium. It wasn't quite how Gareth had imagined things would be in the big leagues.

Or sound like. At half-time in the tiny dressing room, the Palace team were screamed and shouted at. Gareth couldn't believe the way the coaches spoke to the players, and how much they swore!

It was just as tough on the field. The plays were fast and intense. It was his first real taste of the professional game. Gareth only played for ten minutes, but he learned a valuable lesson: at every game at this level, he would be challenged like never before. So he had to be ready for anything.

Gareth played fifteen times in that fast, furious and physical league. And by then, Palace had seen enough. They wanted to sign him full-time as an apprentice. "Go away and think about it," he was told.

SIGNING ON

There was no thinking needed from sixteen-year-old Gareth. He had made his mind up. He was desperate to be a footballer. His mum and dad were not so sure.

His mum wanted him to stay on at school, take his A Levels and get some qualifications in case football didn't work out. His dad was more on his side, saying, "This could be your only chance."

Gareth had done very well at school in his O Levels. (These were exams which were later changed to GCSEs.) He got eight passes, which proved that he was really smart.

His parents left the final decision to Gareth. So he signed for the club, on a wage of £27.50 a week. He soon realized he had made the right decision. In the apprentice squad, there were two players who had decided to carry on their schooling instead of focusing a hundred per cent on football, and they were treated as outsiders. Coaches didn't think they were as committed so if Gareth had been studying as well, he might have been overlooked.

Apprentices have to do all the mucky jobs. Toilet cleaning, boot cleaning and floor cleaning. The kids who were still at school were let off such boring, dirty work. But when it came to picking the team, the coaches had an excuse not to pick the kids still in education because there was a sense that those players didn't need success as much. They had schooling to fall back on. And those two players weren't too bothered, either.

BEST MATES

When training for the youth team at Crystal Palace, Gareth would often run the risk of being late. A game of pool with his great friend Andy Woodman would often go on too long due to the pair's competitive spirit. They are still friends to this day.

And boy, was it a test in that Palace youth set-up. The dressing-room showers were never hot, always cold, and there were thirty of the lads crammed in there. "The conditions were poor," admitted Alan Smith, the manager. But they were supposed to be. It was meant to be hard to show who could be tough enough to get through it.

At the start of each season, the players were all packed off to an army training camp. They would train with the soldiers, grown men who weren't afraid to be rough and tough on the pitch. Gareth and his teammates were woken at 6 a.m. by a bugle, then they would run until they dropped.

WAKE-UP CALL

It was only two months into his apprenticeship that Gareth got into hot water with Alan Smith. He had injured his leg in a tackle and had a deep cut running the length of his shin. He needed six stitches.

The team were losing games heavily. The players were unhappy and training was not enjoyable. Gareth was asked to go to see the manager in his office. He was told to sit down. Smith said: "I'm going to tell you how you are doing."

Gareth was expecting to be told that he was doing okay; there was room for improvement but his attitude was good and he worked hard. Instead,

Smith started shouting and swearing.

Gareth was told he wouldn't have been playing even if he hadn't been injured. He was mentally weak. He was physically weak. And he was dropped from the team line-up.

The tears welled in Gareth's eyes. But Smith didn't end there.

"You're no good to this club, no good to yourself, no good to anyone. When you came I had high hopes but you'd be better off as a travel agent. Footballer? No chance!"

The tears poured down Gareth's face as he left the training ground for home. But he realized he had given himself an excuse. He knew that because he was smart, he wouldn't have any trouble getting a job. If football didn't work out he could go and try something else. Alan Smith had realized that, too.

The next game was against Oxford United and Palace lost 6–2. Gareth sat in the dressing room in his blazer and grey trousers, thinking he would be spared the post-game dressing-down from Alan.

I didn't play so he can't blame me, thought Gareth. Each of the players were, in Gareth's words, "absolutely slaughtered" by Alan Smith. Gareth had never heard anything like it. But then Alan turned to Gareth.

"Don't you be sitting there looking smug," he screamed. "You've done nothing at this club. You've got no chance."

Alan ranted and raved for nearly two hours.

This was the harsh, brutal reality of football. Gareth knew he had to toughen up. Strangely, Alan would go on to become Gareth's mentor and one of the most important people in his life. He said the things he did because he was wanted Gareth to improve. Gareth realized Alan was actually trying to help. Mind you, the Palace youth team lost the next game 7–0 to Northampton!

Slowly but surely, Gareth improved. He started to play at right-back. He then graduated from the youth team to the reserves. This meant he would play on a Saturday morning for the youth team and then again in the afternoon for the reserves. That would never happen today with young players considered multi-million pound assets who are in danger of burnout from too many matches.

OUTSIDER

Gareth struggled to fit in with the other youth team players. He was considered different. For a start, he had done very well in his exams and was considered brainier than his teammates. That meant he was looked at with mistrust. He would hear other players whisper about him. "He did well at school, you know." "Yeah, but can he play?"

He didn't have the same family background as many of the others. He came from Crawley, a quiet, respectable new town thirty miles from London. A lot of his teammates were streetwise inner-city lads. They spoke differently, behaved differently. They were cocky and confident and always making jokes. And they dressed differently. They were trendy. Gareth was not. In fact, Gareth turned up on his first day as an apprentice wearing his school uniform! He had his tie in his pocket because he wasn't sure what the rules were about how they should be dressed.

Gareth wore clothes his mum had bought him from catalogues and high-street stores. His teammates wore cool tracksuits from Adidas and the latest trainers. And they would make jokes about him behind his back. One day, he walked into the dressing room to see a player called Chris Powell, who was a year older, wearing Gareth's comfortable, sensible shoes, prancing around the dressing room as if he was a ballroom dancer. The other players fell about laughing – until they saw Gareth's face. They hadn't meant to upset him.

Another teammate, Barry Ellis, a centre-back, took Gareth shopping. They bought new shoes and trousers. The next day Gareth turned up and all the players went "wow!" He was beginning to fit in.

The favourite

Gareth was still seen as different, though. It didn't help that Alan Smith, who had given Gareth a terrible telling-off, had now taken him under his wing. He was one of the "manager's favourites", and the other players would make fun of him for that.

To cope, Gareth threw himself into training. At school he had been used to being the fastest, the fittest and, of course, the best footballer. But here it was different. The boys who had already done their first year were unbelievably strong, fast and skilful.

In a twelve-minute run, Chris Powell lapped Gareth, and if you got lapped you had to do extra running. Ouch! Gareth's lungs burned.

There was a lot of running. The young hopefuls had to do cross-country runs and on some days they would be told to do eight 400-metre runs, plus eight 200-metre runs. Gareth went from being at the back of the running group to leading the way. His dedication did not go unnoticed.

PROGRESS

What Gareth realized early on in his apprenticeship at Palace was that everybody could play. What would separate players who would make it from those who would disappear into amateur football or other jobs was attitude. If he worked harder than everyone else, showed more dedication and improved his skills, he would stand the best possible chance of success.

And he was right. It also helped that he was likeable. Gareth didn't show off. He didn't bully people. He wasn't selfish. These were the reasons why Alan Smith would make him captain of the youth team. It was why, when the Crystal Palace first team – who trained next to the reserves – needed an extra player for an eleven-a-side game, Gareth would get called over.

Gareth was "Mr Reliable". So reliable that he played for four seasons in the reserves and totted up 120 matches. He was desperate to go out on loan to another professional club to gain experience. But he was always told: "No Gareth, we need you. What if one of the first team got injured?"

He had to wait his turn. Calmly and patiently, Gareth told himself to be ready for when the call came.

Apprentice Life

Training would start with a twelve-minute run round a 400-metre track. Anyone who got lapped would be told to keep going.

After coaching sessions, often led by Steve Coppell, who would later become a famous manager, the young boys had to clean the first-team players' boots as well as the changing rooms.

They all wore Crystal Palace tracksuits and the conversation rarely changed. "Do you think I'll make it", "Do you think the manager likes me?"

Apprentices earned just £27.50 a week. Games were played on a Saturday morning. If a player was good he played for the reserve team in the afternoon, meaning he would come off ten minutes before the end of the first match and be driven to the reserve game if it was an away match.

BIG CHANCE

Gareth was twenty years old when his time finally came. He had been at Palace for four years and survived Alan Smith's cruel-to-be-kind ways. Later on, that youth apprenticeship scheme came to be known as the Bear Pit, because so few survived it to make a career in football.

The date was 25 September 1990, three weeks after his birthday, and Gareth was picked as a substitute against the "mighty" Southend United in a League Cup game. Okay, it wasn't Manchester United or Liverpool, but Gareth didn't care.

I'm on my way! thought Gareth.

He came off the substitutes' bench to play in an 8–0 victory for his side. Ian Wright, the England striker, and Mark Bright both scored hat-tricks. Gareth had to wait another six months before his next chance came. This time, he played from the start in a 1–1 draw in the Zenith Data Systems Cup. It may not have been a big game in front of a crowd of 30,000, but Gareth didn't mind.

Steve Coppell, a boyhood hero of Gareth's when Coppell played for Manchester United, was the Palace manager. He liked what he saw of Gareth. He knew that Gareth was reliable and honest, and he could play.

Coppell reckoned that it would not be long before he could build a team around this young player who was so cool, calm and collected. But before he did, he wanted to make sure he was ready. Coppell decided to throw Gareth in at the deep end.

RUSH JOB

There was no more intimidating place in world football to make your professional football league debut than Anfield, the home of Liverpool FC. Liverpool were the league champions. They had won eight of the previous twelve titles and they were gunning for another. Liverpool were *the* unstoppable force in English football. They had dominated every team for years. In April 1991, 37,000 fans packed into the famous old ground for the game against Crystal Palace.

The Kop, the huge stand behind the goal which housed Liverpool's most passionate supporters, was scarily loud. The fans were particularly noisy that day as they welcomed the new manager, Graeme Souness. Graeme had replaced the legend that was Kenny Dalgleish.

Just as scary were the brilliant players on the pitch, like John Barnes, Peter Beardsley and Ian Rush.

Thanks, gaffer, thought Gareth as Steve Coppell told him he would be playing because Eric Young and Andy Thorn, two defenders, were both injured.

Gareth would be making his first league start against the trickiest, fastest and most deadly strike trio in the game. As centre-back, it was Gareth's job to stop Barnes, a footballing magician; Beardsley, a fearless runner with the ball; and Rush, a goal-scoring machine.

Gareth was nervous. But as he stood in the tunnel in Palace's away strip of blue shirt (with the number five on his back), shorts and socks with red trim, he took a deep breath and thought to himself: *You've got this. This is what you've trained for. It's just a game of football.*

Gareth, when the pressure was on, went into safe and sensible mode. He wouldn't allow himself to be worried. He looked up at the famous "This is Anfield" sign in the players' tunnel, then walked out into the most magnificent atmosphere.

The TV commentator mentioned him on *Match of the Day*. "Palace give a league debut to twenty-two year old Gareth Southgate, a six-footer from Croydon."

It didn't take long for Gareth to get another mention. The ball was played to Ian Rush and Gareth thought it would be a good idea to "let him know I'm here".

Whack!

Gareth sent the legendary goalscorer flying with a late challenge. Rush landed in a heap. The Kop went crazy. Gareth, nine minutes into his league debut, was shown a yellow card. But he didn't mind. Gareth was letting Rush know that he wouldn't let him out of his sight. He was going to be his shadow.

But Rush was too smart, too experienced. A few minutes later, he got his own back.

Kick!

The striker gave Gareth a sneaky kick after he cleared the ball. A running battle between the wily old fox and the young upstart was really on now.

Gareth was doing well. With the crowd roaring Liverpool on, creating a deafening noise, Rush had a glorious chance to give Liverpool the lead. But just as Rush was about to fire home right-footed in the six-yard box, who made a last-ditch, brilliant tackle to deny him? Gareth!

But it would be a battle Rush would eventually win. Just before half-time, what looked like a harmless ball was played forward by Liverpool. Gareth came out to meet it, thinking he would mop up the ball and start an attack. But Rush had other ideas. He used his body to shepherd Gareth out of the way and turn him inside out in one motion. Gareth ended up on his hands and knees, looking on as Rush exchanged rapid passes with Peter Beardsley.

"See you later, son!" Rush seemed to say to Gareth.

Gareth was back on his feet in time to see Rush slam a shot past the Palace goalkeeper for his 300th goal in club football.

Liverpool went on to win the game 3–0. But Gareth, not one to get carried away, noted that he had done okay. Steve Coppell thought the same. He thought he had a player on his hands.

In fact, Coppell had several players on his hands. Gareth was not the only youngster to impress him. Richard Shaw, John Salako, Simon Osbourn and Geoff Thomas, all products of the Bear Pit, also played in that game. They were Crystal Palace's bright young things and the following season, with Gareth leading the way, they would return to Anfield and win 2–1, with Gareth keeping a certain Mr Rush quiet throughout the game.

STEPPING UP

Despite just three appearances for Crystal Palace's first team, Gareth now felt that he belonged. And his teammates felt the same way, too. As a sign that he was one of them, he even had a nickname. Gareth was called "Nord".

This was after a TV presenter at the time, called Dennis Norden, who hosted a show of celebrities' bloopers and mistakes. Norden spoke very carefully and pronounced every word perfectly. The Palace dressing room noticed that whenever Gareth opened his mouth, even to give a senior player advice (what confidence!) that he made sure every word was said correctly, too. He also looked a bit like Norden, awkward and with a long nose!

Gareth didn't mind. He felt comfortable now and his teammates were comfortable with him. They knew he could play, of course. They also saw a ridiculously calm young player who, in the heat of the game, could make clear, clever decisions. They noticed how he always wanted to learn. He was like a sponge for knowledge, someone who would always be asking questions and giving opinions.

"What do I do here?"

"How do I play against this striker?"

"Maybe we should try this?"

EARNING HIS KEEP

After his Liverpool game, Gareth spent the summer break asking more questions, studying how teams played, assessing the strengths and weaknesses of opposition players. He wanted to kick on and make himself a regular player. He wanted to be someone who was undroppable.

The 1991–92 season would prove to be the making of Gareth. He played thirty times, only four of those as a substitute coming off the bench. He played at centre-back, right-back and in midfield. He was fast becoming Palace's "Mr Reliable" – someone who Coppell knew could do a job any time, and anywhere on the field.

There was no doubt Gareth had made it. His dream of becoming a professional had come true. He would have a career in the game. Did he celebrate? Of course not. That wasn't his style.

Gareth was different. He rejected the so-called "footballer's lifestyle" of driving flashy cars and splashing his cash around.

It was typical of Gareth that he instead chose to work part-time in Palace's marketing team, helping to bring revenue into the club. He had a third job, too. He wrote a weekly column for the local newspaper. And that didn't mean a journalist phoning him up, asking questions, then writing the article for him. No way. Gareth would go down to the newspaper offices, sit at a desk and write it himself.

Palace finished tenth in the division that season. It was the last season before what was known as the First Division became the Premiership and a new era of English football began.

Premier League

The Premier League is the highest league in professional football in England. It is the most famous league in the world. It has twenty clubs. The team that finishes in first position are called the champions of England. The teams that finish in the bottom three are relegated to the league below, the Championship. The season runs from August to May, unless the football season is disrupted by a pandemic or the Winter World Cup, and each club plays the others twice: at home and away.

GOALSCORER

The 1992–93 season was historic in English football. The Premiership, later to be called the Premier League, was born. It was more than a change of name. Football in England had often been seen as unfashionable, but the Premiership was full of glitz and glamour. Huge transfer deals brought the biggest players in the world to play in the league. Matches were shown live on TV every week. It was all anyone talked about.

Gareth, "Mr Reliable", wasn't the poster boy for the new league. But he was an up-and-coming young talent and wise beyond his years. And, guess what? He started this new era by smashing in goals for Palace.

In the first match of the season against Blackburn Rovers at home, Gareth scored a stunner. A corner was not cleared properly and the ball fell to Gareth about twenty-five yards out. He steadied himself, swung his right foot and hit the ball on the bounce...

Thwack!

The ball went straight into the top corner. Gareth was mobbed by his teammates. It was his first goal for the club – and what a way to get it!

Unfortunately, Palace couldn't win the game. They drew 3–3. It was a sign of things to come. Palace had plenty of flair and pace, but they leaked goals at the back. Wins were hard to come by.

THE DROP

Gareth scored his second goal in December but by then, Palace were bottom of the league and fighting for survival. It came in a 2–0 home win against Sheffield United and this win sparked the team into life. They won the next four games, beating Queens Park Rangers, Leeds, Wimbledon and Middlesbrough. They even beat Liverpool in the League Cup. Suddenly, Palace had dreams of avoiding relegation.

But then Gareth got injured and the team's recovery stalled. Gareth had to watch from the stands in physical and mental anguish as Palace slid towards the trapdoor. He returned at right-back in March, scoring against Nottingham Forest. But Palace won only three of their next eleven matches and were relegated to the lower division.

Gareth took it hard. He took it personally. He felt like a failure. And to this day, he says that the horrible feeling of relegation never leaves you. It is made harder when the manager loses his job because of it. Steve Coppell was replaced as Palace manager.

The new manager would be the perfect fit for Gareth. He had been there at Gareth's previous lowest moment in football. Now he was back in Gareth's life again. Alan Smith was now in charge.

Hard on Himself

On New Years' Eve 1994 in a match against Blackburn Rovers, Gareth was in midfield for Crystal Palace. A mistake he made led to a goal and Palace lost 1–0. Gareth couldn't get over it. All his teammates went out to celebrate the New Year, but he stayed at home and relived the goal over and over in his head.

SKIPPER

Alan Smith had always treated Gareth like a son. From those days when he asked Gareth to come and help him out in the garden, to driving him back from training in his Jaguar or dishing out tellings-off because he cared so much, the two were close.

So it was no surprise that with Alan looking to put his own stamp on the Palace team as they looked to return immediately to the Premiership, he made Gareth captain. A couple of senior players were injured and Alan needed a new leader. For him, there could be only one choice.

At twenty-three and with barely a full

season under his belt, could Gareth boss around experienced, tough and arrogant senior players? Not a problem. From an early age, Gareth had the respect of everyone. They knew that he knew what he was talking about. It is that quality that he took through into management years later.

Promotion!

Under Gareth's leadership, Palace swept all before them. He was their midfield dynamo – passing, running, tacking, shouting and organizing. Sometimes he seemed to win games on his own by the sheer force of his personality and his ability to get players to do that extra bit for the team.

Of course there were other superstars, too. Chris Coleman was the centre-half. Yep, the same Chris Coleman who would manage Wales to the semi-finals of the European Championships in 2016.

There was Chris Armstrong, too. He scored an incredible twenty-four goals in that season and was one of the hottest strikers in Europe. But the man second to him on the Palace goalscoring lists was something of an eyebrow-raiser. Yes, it was Gareth! He scored twelve goals that season, including a humdinger from thirty yards against Portsmouth. In their last-but-one game of the season, Palace beat Middlesbrough 3–2 to win promotion. Typically, Gareth got the first goal. He became Palace's youngest-ever promotion skipper!

STRAIGHT BACK DOWN

Palace's first game of the new season in the Premiership was against Liverpool at home. It wasn't as scary as it sounded. Liverpool were not the unbeatable force they had been, and were entering a long period of disappointment at their inability to challenge for the league title.

But even a weakened Liverpool were too much for the newcomers – they lost the game 6–1. By half time, they were already 3–0 down. Gareth playing in midfield with Ray Wilkins, the former England international thought: *Oh no! Here we go again...*

He was right. Palace were out of their depth.

Again. The club had another horrible season. They won only one of their first ten games, a shock success at Arsenal.

Gareth was still learning, though. The previous season he had relished playing with Wilkins and picked his brains on everything about football. How best to prepare, train or eat. When Palace went on away trips, he would stay in the same hotel room as Wilkins and they would just talk about football for hours and hours. Alan Smith had told the pair to room together.

"Help this one," Alan said to Ray Wilkins. "He's going places."

Unfortunately, Ray broke his foot in that game against Liverpool, robbing Palace of their midfield dream team. Ray was a huge influence on Gareth's career and years later in 2018, when Ray died suddenly, Gareth was devastated.

CUP RUNS

Gareth played all forty-two league games that season. There was brief hope of avoiding another grim relegation battle. They won four in a row in between 22 October and 5 November, but, to be truthful, Gareth knew that the fixture list had been kind. The teams they beat were Wimbledon, Leicester City, Coventry City and Ipswich Town. Hardly a "Who's Who" of Premiership best teams. As soon as Palace came up against stronger opposition, they were in trouble again. Towards the end of November, Manchester United burst their bubble, beating them 3–0.

It was hugely frustrating for Gareth. *Why can't we do it when it really counts?* he thought. He was right to wonder. Palace were poor in the league, but in the cup competitions they were brilliant. They couldn't stop winning.

Crystal Palace were the lowest scorers in the Premiership that season, with thirty-four goals in forty-two games. But in cup games, they scored twenty-seven goals in fifteen matches.

Gareth thought long and hard about why Palace could succeed in games which, frankly, didn't matter as much. Maybe it was the pressure? Premiership survival was everything. Many of the players had come through the youth teams under Alan Smith. Could their desperation to achieve success for him be causing the physical and mental tension that was holding back their performance? And did this experience impact Gareth's own managerial plans later on his career, when he tried really hard to make players relax?

In the cup matches, Palace played without fear. Crystal Palace made it to the semi-final of the League Cup and faced Liverpool. The first leg was played away at Anfield. Palace only lost 1–0, keeping their hopes of going to Wembley alive. But in the home leg at Selhurst Park, they were beaten again, by the same scoreline.

Palace also got through to the semi-final of the FA Cup, against Manchester United. The match was a draw, and the replay was memorable for Gareth having an incredible tussle with one of the most competitive and fierce midfield players in history.

HARD MAN

Roy Keane is a TV pundit these days. He is known for his fiery attitude and forthright views and is always ready to "tell it like it is". If a team or player is not trying hard enough or is playing badly, Keane says so. He doesn't care if he upsets anyone. So just imagine what he was like to play against!

Keane was one of the most frightening players ever. He slammed into tackles. *Whack!* He barged players out of the way. *Thump!* And sometimes he went too far, committing fouls and getting involved in arguments that sometimes turned into fights.

But Gareth wasn't scared of Keane. He relished

their physical battles in the middle of the pitch. Why? Because Gareth was similar to Keane. He loved the tough tackling and the aggression. It was part of his game. He just didn't lose his cool as often as Keane did. And do you know what? Keane respected him for it. He now says Gareth was a "top man" for the way he played the game and how he behaved off the pitch.

That is hard to believe given that the pair had one of the most memorable on-field clashes in football history.

The first semi-final, played at Aston Villa's Villa Park, was a thriller that ended in a 2–2 draw. The rematch was only memorable because it was Gareth vs. Roy Keane. Palace were 2–0 down at the time and the game was petering out. There was a loose ball near the halfway line and Gareth and Keane both went towards it. All hell was about to break loose.

Keane, for some reason, saw red. He narrowly missed chopping down Gareth with a wild and high tackle as the ball bounced. Gareth knew that Keane had set out to foul him and he saw red, too. As the ball rolled towards the touchline, Gareth launched himself at Keane.

Smash!

Gareth dived two-footed long after the ball had gone into Keane, committing the sort of foul that would have seen him handed a red card in the modern game. Keane was furious. He hammered his foot down into Gareth's chest not once, but twice.

Stamp! Stamp!

Gareth doubled up in pain. Then the other United and Palace players started pushing and fighting. It was pandemonium! Keane was immediately sent off. United managed to hold on without conceding a goal, meaning that the night was doubly painful for Gareth.

These days, Gareth and Keane can laugh about it. The pair were both TV pundits for Chelsea and Manchester City's FA Cup semi-final in 2013. During the match, Sergio Aguero, the City striker, stamped on David Luiz, which brought back a few memories.

"That was the worst challenge in an FA Cup semi-final since Roy's," Gareth chuckled. Keane, jokingly, always uses Gareth's tackle as an example as to why defenders must stay on their feet.

And so Palace's dreams of a Wembley final were dashed, and their dreams of staying in the Premiership went the same way. Palace were back in the first division. They were something of a joke, too, with opposing fans laughing at them and calling them a "yo-yo" club, one which would come up and go straight back down again.

Gareth had so desperately wanted to help Palace keep their place in the top flight for Alan Smith, his mentor and friend. But Alan lost his job and it was the end of an era.

A VILLAIN

Gareth was almost twenty-five years old, and nearing his peak as a player. He needed to progress. In all, he had played 191 games and scored twenty-two goals for Palace. But he wanted to win trophies and he wanted to play for England. He just didn't think any of that was possible if he stayed at Palace. After the relegation, the club chairman, Ron Noades, agreed that he would listen to offers for their star player. Palace needed the money, too, and they had got eight years' worth of valuable service from Gareth.

Quickly, Aston Villa made their interest known.

They were a huge club, with great potential to challenge for trophies.

Yes, thought Gareth. *Villa is my sort of club.*

He travelled up by train from London to Birmingham to sign the contract. What would follow was one of the more bizarre moments in his career. The Villa chairman was a businessman called Doug Ellis. He was nicknamed "Deadly" because he liked to fire managers. He had a reputation for being difficult to deal with and for getting exactly what he wanted.

Doug Ellis walked into the meeting room where Gareth and his new manager, Brian Little, were waiting. Doug was wearing a Hawaiian shirt. *What is going on here?* Gareth thought.

Doug looked through the contract. He nodded, then handed it to Gareth to sign. But then Doug said he would have to call the Palace chairman, Ron Noades. Despite Gareth having signed the contract and legally becoming a Villa player, Doug told Ron that his new signing was asking for too much money in wages. And he needed some cash taken off the transfer fee which had already been agreed.

He started by asking for £100,000 off. Ron was

furious as Doug laughed to himself. Eventually, Doug managed to get £50,000 off the agreed fee. Palace sold Gareth to Aston Villa for £2.5 million. The phone call cost Ron £50,000. Doug didn't really care about saving this relatively small amount – he just wanted to get one up on his rival, Ron Noades.

Gareth thought this was strange behaviour, and he didn't think it was a good sign. He had joined Villa because Doug had convinced him that the club had big ambitions. But if Doug was prepared to be small-minded like that, could he really be trusted?

Gareth put it to the back of his mind. *Just concentrate on the football,* he told himself. And, boy, what football! Villa started the season brilliantly. On the opening day of the season, they thrashed Manchester United 3–1! They won six of their first ten matches, losing just once. It was a far cry from Gareth's struggles with Palace the previous season.

Gareth was asked to play at centre-back instead of in the midfield. He lined up beside Ugo Ehiogu, who would go on to play for England, and Paul McGrath, who was the star of Ireland's World Cup finals campaign in 1994.

The three men were a defensive mean machine.

They worked so well together, it was like magic. If one of them had the ball, the other two knew exactly what he was going to do with it. They knew exactly where the others were in terms of position, where they were going to run, or when they were going to tackle or block. They could almost have played together with their eyes closed.

"It's easy," Gareth said when asked how he coped with playing against some of the Premiership's most fearsome strikers. McGrath said it was "effortless". It is perhaps no wonder that Gareth has always preferred the three-at-the-back defensive system as a manager. It comes directly from that first season he played at Villa.

Gareth's form was so good that soon, England came calling.

ENGLAND CALL-UP

When he was twelve years old, Gareth had the full England kit – the one they wore in the 1982 World Cup. He would put on the shirt, shorts and socks and pretend he was Bryan Robson, the Manchester United midfielder and England captain. Robson was his hero. It was why Gareth started out playing in midfield. He wanted to be just like Robson and play for his country.

But Gareth kept this dream to himself. He thought if he told other players about it that they'd laugh or say that he wasn't good enough. Even his great friend, goalkeeper Andy Woodman, felt that

Gareth would never play for England. He was wrong.

The call came for England's match against Portugal in December 1995. Terry Venables was the manager. It was just a friendly match because England had automatically qualified for the following year's European Championships because the tournament was being held in England. If Gareth could perform well in this match, he might get a place in the squad for the first major tournament held in England since the 1966 World Cup.

Before matches, the England squad stayed at the Burnham Beeches hotel in Berkshire. It was a huge, grand hotel with swimming pools, a golf course and extensive grounds. Gareth couldn't believe his eyes!

"If you ever stay at Burnham Beeches," he said, "You've made it."

On his first day at the hotel, there was a knock on his room door. He opened it to find all his England training kit neatly laid out for him. He felt like a kid again. Excitedly, he tried on the kit in front of the mirror! He was so excited, he almost forgot there was an actual game to play.

Gareth started the game as a substitute. And would you believe, he almost scored within seconds of coming off the bench! His header whacked into the crossbar and would have been the winner, but Portugal equalized and the match finished 1–1.

A day in the Life of an England International

You're picked up from home in a chauffer-driven car and taken to the five-star team hotel. You don't need to check in – that's been done for you.

If it's a major tournament, waiting in your room are expensive gifts from sponsors, such as clothes and sometimes a set of golf clubs in case you've forgotten yours. In Gareth's time, there was a free laptop, DVDs to watch and CDs to listen to. And an envelope with £60 cash to spend.

Everything from drinks, to meals and laundry, is paid for.

Travelling to a game abroad, you fly business class, having been driven directly to the plane steps. At the destination, you don't have to queue for passport checks or wait for your luggage. That's already in your room when you get there.

SILVERWARE

Gareth was living the dream. He was an England player, Villa had a superb season in the league (they would finish fourth, with Manchester United as the champions), and he had established himself as a brilliant centre back. Villa were even in the race for a trophy.

It was the League Cup again, the competition in which Palace had come so close. Villa breezed through to the semi-final, beating Wolves, Queens Park Rangers (QPR), Stockport and Peterborough. They barely broke a sweat in fact.

The two-leg semi-final was different, however.

They would have to overcome Arsenal, who had stars like Dutch legend Dennis Bergkamp.

Halfway through the first leg, Villa looked done for. They were two goals down with Bergkamp netting twice. However, Dwight Yorke, Villa's own super striker, scored two and the match ended in a 2–2 draw.

The second leg ended 0–0. Yorke's goals in the first leg proved crucial because, instead of the match being decided on penalties, Villa were the winners as they had scored more away goals than Arsenal! The "away goals" rule rewarded teams for attacking in away legs to stop matches being boring.

Villa had made it to Wembley! The final against Leeds was a bit of an anti-climax. It was just too easy for Villa, particularly Gareth. His battle with the powerful and skilful striker Tony Yeboa was where the match would be won and lost. Thanks to Gareth, Yeboah never had a sniff at goal.

Savo Milosevic, who had been cruelly nicknamed Savo "Miss-a-lot-evic", because he had struggled in front of the goal, scored a brilliant opener. He got another and then set up Yorke for the third.

It was Gareth's first trophy as a professional. He

celebrated by dancing around and singing in the dressing room and drinking champagne from the trophy itself!

He was a Wembley winner. In just a few months, though, he would go home with very different memories of the place.

EURO 96

The European Championships in 1996 in England provided a lifetime of memories for football fans. The whole country was behind England, who seemed to be getting better and better with each game as they progressed into the knockout stages.

For those too young to remember it, it was exactly like the summer of 2021 when England, under the managership of a certain Gareth Southgate, came so close to glory.

Back in '96, Gareth was the mainstay of England's defence. He started every single game. He was solid against Switzerland, Scotland and the

Netherlands in the group stage. The Netherlands match was probably one of England's greatest performances. Although the Dutch were supposedly the better team, England thrashed them 4–1.

Gareth and England were riding the crest of a wave. They felt unstoppable. Although tucked away at Burnham Beeches hotel again, they could feel the atmosphere building each time they took the coach to Wembley for a game. Each time, it felt like more and more fans were with them.

Amazingly, Gareth was not only finding his feet at international level but with his teammates, too. He had worried that Paul Gascoigne would make fun of him – but it didn't happen. He was worried that hardman Stuart Pearce would think he was "soft". After Gareth crunched him in a tackle in training, that didn't happen either.

Gareth and the other England players had to work out a kind of rota system to keep brilliant but unpredictable striker Paul Gascoigne occupied. Table tennis, snooker, badminton, cards – everyone had to take their turn to look after the player.

Gareth made defending against Europe's best players look so easy. In the quarter-final against

Spain, he was unruffled, even though Spain seemed to have so much more of the ball. He didn't put a foot wrong. He was so good he was almost forgotten because he made everything he did look so simple.

After a draw at ninety minutes, England beat Spain on penalties to set up a semi-final against Germany, England's old rivals.

AGONY

At full time, the match against Germany was 1–1. Gareth felt that England could and should have won it, but they didn't and the match would now be decided on penalties. On the final whistle, he felt a strange sense of relief.

It's out of my hands now, thought Gareth. He was wrong.

Gareth was asked if he would take a penalty. He said yes. Bryan Robson, his hero, who was a coach with the England team, asked him whether he'd taken one before. Gareth said yes. He was telling the truth – sort of. He didn't tell Robson that he had only taken one for Palace, and had missed, hitting the post against Ipswich.

What he remembers most is the silence as he walked to take England's sixth penalty. Then the England fans started clapping him. He wanted to put it to the left. But the goalkeeper Andreas Kopke saw him look at his target. Gareth panicked.

Put it to the right, then, he thought to himself. *No, stick to the left. Never change your mind.*

The silence returned when Gareth ran up to the ball. It was badly hit. Badly placed. Kopke saved easily. The air was filled with anguish. England were knocked out as soon as Andreas Müller dispatched Germany's winning kick.

BELT IT

As a kid Gareth practised penalties for hour after hour in his back garden. His mum would have to call him for his dinner as it got dark. He would tell his mum, "If ever I take an important penalty, I'm going to blast it."

After the game, his mum was one of the first people he spoke to. "You always said you were going to belt it," she reminded him.

In the days afterwards, newspaper reporters kept ringing Gareth's mum and dad and knocking on their door, wanting to know if they had spoken to Gareth. His parents had never dealt with the media before. Unfortunately, Barbara told them about the phone conversation. And the next day the front pages were full of headlines like: "Southgate's mum: 'Why didn't you just belt it?'"

Barbara was upset for days. But Gareth didn't mind. He tried to tell her it didn't matter and that was just the way things were. But since then, Barbara has never spoken to another journalist.

VILLAIN AGAIN

The new football season couldn't come soon enough for Gareth. He thought about that penalty miss a lot. And wherever he went, people asked about it. It followed him around like a black cloud. His only escape was on the pitch. He was desperate to get out there and play again and make happier memories.

Gareth had good reason to believe the 1996–97 season would help. Could Aston Villa build on last season's fourth-placed finish, and do well in the UEFA Cup, which they had qualified for by winning the League Cup?

Unfortunately they couldn't. Villa finished fifth

in the Premier League and, embarrassingly, went out of the UEFA Cup in the first round against Helsingborgs, a small Swedish team.

The next season was another disappointment. Gareth was made captain, which he was pleased about. The captain's spot had been created when Andy Townsend moved to Middlesbrough. Townsend had been a key player in the Villa team, and Gareth was beginning to get frustrated by the club's lack of ambition in signing big-name players. There was no sign of Villa closing the gap on the best teams in the league and challenging for the title.

Gareth felt badly let down. He had been made promises that Villa were a club that was going places, and they weren't. They were treading water, going nowhere.

Speaking Out

Gareth wasn't keen on the signing of his former Palace teammate, Stan Collymore. Gareth knew that the striker would not train hard and could "go missing" in games, and he was not afraid to say so.

Gareth caused another row at Villa by telling a newspaper reporter that the club wasn't ambitious enough. Brian Little, the Villa manager, was furious, and hit back at Gareth in the media. The Villa dressing room was not a great place to be and soon, results started to suffer.

Villa's best hope of a trophy was in the UEFA Cup again but, just before their big match against Atlético Madrid in the fourth round, Brian Little resigned as manager. He was replaced by the coach, John Gregory. Villa lost the two-leg tie and went out of the competition.

In the league, they finished seventh. They were getting worse! And Gareth knew it.

The next season, even though they started brilliantly, winning nine of their first twelve games in all competitions – Gareth knew that it was a fluke. The team didn't train hard enough and there were too few players who did the right things off the pitch.

SMILE FOR THE CAMERA

Again, Gareth didn't see eye-to-eye with his manager, John Gregory. When Villa won 4–1 at Southampton to make it twelve league games unbeaten, Gregory said there should be a team photo on the pitch to celebrate. Gareth couldn't believe it.

"Why? We haven't won anything yet! That's embarrassing!"

Everywhere Villa went after that, opposition players and managers would bring it up, mocking them. Alan Shearer, the England striker, said to Gareth: "Team photo, eh?" as if to say "What were you playing at?"

Despite Villa being top of the league in November, Gareth knew it couldn't last. Eventually, they were found out and could finish only sixth – a massive twenty points off the third spot. It was the beginning of the end of Gareth's Villa career.

The next season, Gareth asked for a transfer. His request was rejected and he was reminded he was under contract and going nowhere. Doug Ellis, the chairman, assured Gareth that he had plenty of ambition for the club. He told Gareth that he had tried to buy Frank Lampard and Freddie Kanoute from West Ham for a combined fee of £5 million. Lampard was eventually sold to Chelsea for £10 million on his own and Gareth remembered that phone call Doug had made to Ron Noades when he signed Gareth from Palace.

It was an upsetting time for Gareth. He wanted to leave. He had given Villa good performances for years and, to make it worse, the Villa supporters thought he was betraying them. It was nonsense. Gareth continued to give his all, despite being denied the chance of a move to Chelsea or Spanish club Deportivo La Coruña.

An FA Cup final was the one bright spot in

the 1999–2000 season. But guess what? Villa were
beaten by Chelsea 1–0 with Gareth being involved
in a mix-up with keeper David James and conceding
the goal. He needed to get away from Villa.

BORO BOUND

In July 2001, Gareth finally got his move and joined Middlesbrough (Boro) for a transfer fee of £6.5 million. It was a surprising move – this was Gareth's last big chance to achieve big things but Boro had never won a major trophy.

What convinced him to go there was the promises he received of investment in the team, and the chance to work with Steve McClaren, a coach he had worked with in the England squad. He would also join up again with his old Villa centre-back partner Ugo Ehiogu.

With Gareth on board, Boro did well. They made

it to the semi-final of the FA Cup and finished twelfth in the Premier League. Gareth was named Player of the Season. More importantly, big players were arriving. Geremi, the Cameroon international, came from Real Madrid. And, best of all, Juninho, the Brazilian midfield wizard, returned to the club.

This is what I came for, thought Gareth.

By October of the next season, Boro, Juninho and Gareth, made captain when Paul Ince left, were flying. They were third in the league!

But it would be the same old story. Middlesbrough fell away to finish eleventh in 2002–03. Aston Villa, by the way, were sixteenth.

MORE SILVERWARE!

Just when Gareth was starting to reckon that his chance of winning any more silverware was disappearing, Boro splashed the cash in the 2003–04 season. Barcelona players Gaizka Mendieta and Bolo Zenden joined Juninho in the midfield! It was one of the best trios the league had seen at that point.

Gareth was in such great form that there were rumours of a move to Manchester United, who desperately needed a centre-back. It wasn't to be. Meanwhile, Boro were brilliant in the League Cup and knocked out the Arsenal "Invincibles" on their way to the final. (The team got their nickname because they went on to win the league that season without losing a single game.)

In the final, Middlesbrough were too good for Bolton. Gareth was described as a "tower of strength" and, as he lifted the trophy following a 2–1 win, all of Gareth's frustrations came out.

"Yeeeeesssss!" he yelled.

Gareth was happy at Boro. They had kept their promises. And although the League Cup win was not a Champions League winners' medal or a League title, Gareth felt that his desire to leave Villa had been proved right.

He was proved even more right when, two seasons later in 2006, Boro with Gareth found themselves in the final of the UEFA Cup following a rollercoaster campaign with last-gasp goals and brilliant comebacks galore.

Sadly, Middlesbrough were outclassed by Spanish club Sevilla. At the final in Eindhoven, Netherlands, they lost 4–0. It was Gareth's 699th professional appearance. Not bad for someone who was told he had "no chance" of making it and should have been a travel agent instead. The Seville final was his last game as a player. He was thirty-five years old.

ENGLAND DAYS

After 1996, Gareth's England career never hit the same highs again, and he admits now that he never quite got over that penalty miss. His form for his country didn't match his performances for his club, and his place in the team became less certain as younger and quicker players came on the scene, like Rio Ferdinand and Sol Campbell.

However, Gareth still played a crucial role in helping England qualify for the 1998 World Cup. They needed to avoid defeat in Rome against the mighty Italy, otherwise they wouldn't have made it to the World Cup finals, and Gareth was a rock.

That night, England got the draw they needed and on the same pitch as legendary defenders like Paolo Maldini, Gareth matched them and went on to join the team at the 1998 tournament in France.

Gareth started the first match against Tunisia, which England won 2–0, but he didn't make another appearance until he came off the bench in the first knockout round against Argentina. England thought they had a great chance of going far in the tournament under Glenn Hoddle's management. But guess what? They lost on penalties to Argentina. Gareth was ready and willing to take another if required.

Altogether, Gareth played fifty-seven times for England. He scored two goals. His last appearance was against Sweden in Gothenburg in 2004. He captained his country three times. He is Aston Villa's most capped England player. And to think he used to stand in front of the mirror as a twelve-year-old imagining he had Three Lions on his chest for real. Amazing!

Scoring for England

Gareth scored two goals for England. His first goal came on 14 October 1998 against Luxembourg in a Euro 2000 qualifier, his second on 22 May 2003 against South Africa in a friendly.

BOSS

In June 2006, When the manager's job at Middlesbrough came up it didn't seem possible that Gareth would be in with a chance. There were some really big names in the running, like Terry Venables, Martin O'Neill and Alan Curbishley. Another strong candidate was Tony Mowbray, a former Boro player, who had done brilliantly managing Hibernian FC in the Scottish Premier League.

For a start, Gareth wasn't actually qualified. To be a manager, you have to pass your coaching exams and Gareth hadn't taken them yet – he was only thirty-five, and had only recently retired as a player.

But he was the man Boro wanted, and the club persuaded the Premier League to waive the rules.

Gareth's first task was to remind his former teammates that he was now the boss. He used to be one of them, part of the dressing room. Suddenly, he was in charge and he had to tell his old friends what to do. This wasn't easy.

Some players just couldn't bring themselves to call him "gaffer", the nickname for managers in English football. Most kept calling him "Gate". (The "Nord" nickname had long been forgotten.)

Luckily Ray Parlour, the experienced former Arsenal man, gave Gareth an early chance to show who was boss. Parlour joked: "Can't I just call you Big Nose?" Parlour never played for Boro again.

Gareth was exactly the same kind of manager as he was a player. He didn't get over-excited, he remained calm and made sensible decisions. If a player did something wrong, he didn't scream and shout. He carefully and quietly explained what had gone wrong.

Amazingly, his first game in charge of Boro was against Reading who were managed by none other than Steve Coppell, his first Crystal Palace manager. Reading won the game 3–2, and Gareth's inexperience as a manager showed.

The older players noticed in that first season that Gareth wasn't quite sure how to change games if they weren't going his way. But he was learning. In his first season, Boro finished twelfth, an improvement of two places on the previous season. The next season they came thirteenth. Gareth was doing well.

SACKED

Gareth had an almost impossible job. Boro were losing money. They had to sell big players to reduce their wage bill, and there wasn't a lot of money to buy new players.

Out of the door went important players like striker Mark Viduka, powerful Nigerian forward Yakubu, former Real Madrid defender Jonathan Woodgate, Australian goalkeeper Mark Schwarzer and the experienced George Boateng. Gareth lost almost all his best players!

In his third season, in 2008–09, Gareth had to rely on young players. Although they were talented, they didn't have the know-how for the toughest league in the world. The team struggled badly, even though Gareth won a Manager of the Month award early in the season.

But after that, Boro went on a fourtheen–match run without a win and relegation was inevitable. Boro had been in the top league for eleven years.

In 2009–10, Gareth started life well in the Championship. Boro won five of their first seven matches. When they beat Derby County in October they were fourth and a point off the league leaders.

After the game, Gareth celebrated with a drink with his coaches.

"Yes, we're going places," they all agreed.

Gareth went to see the Middlesbrough chairman in the boardroom and wondered whether this was the best time to ask for a new striker, to help out his young team. But instead of getting the green light for that player, he was sacked.

Gareth was shocked, upset and extremely angry. The team were doing well and he was getting better as a manager!

He returned home late that night and, at 1 a.m., he started to make a list of things he had to return to the club. His wife came downstairs.

"They haven't sacked you have they?" she joked.

"Actually, they have. Too nice..."

"Too nice."

After three-and-half years at Middlesbrough and having passed his coaching exams, Gareth didn't think it would be long before he found another job. He was not wrong.

He got a role at the Football Association (FA) as the head of elite development. This meant it was his job to find ways to make players better – how to train for maximum fitness; the best ways to recover from matches; the healthiest foods to eat.

He was brilliant at this job – so good, in fact, that the FA wanted to make him their technical director, and really focus on the football side of things. But Gareth wanted the buzz of being a boss again. So he left the FA.

He applied for several managerial jobs in Championship – but to his disappointment, sometimes he didn't even get a reply. It seemed like no one wanted to know him. When a job came up at Sheffield United, Gareth thought he was in with a great chance. He knew a lot of the people there because some of them sent their children to the same school as he did.

United are the perfect fit for me, he thought.

Gareth did his homework on the club and the squad. "The interview went well," he told his wife, but he didn't get it. He couldn't believe it. What had he done wrong? Why did they not want him? When he found out, he laughed to himself. They said he was "too nice"! Gareth had heard that before when he started his Palace youth career. Gareth had heard this time and again through his career – and every time, he had proved his critics wrong.

It is forgotten that in the whirlwind of success that followed for England that Gareth Southgate only got the national team manager's job because of a crazy incident.

In 2016, England's new manager, Sam Allardyce, was sacked after he spoke to an undercover journalist about breaking transfer rules. England were in crisis. There were no obvious candidates for the manager's job. After the scandal, they needed a manager who was safe, reliable and trustworthy. Nice, maybe?

Gareth got the job and returned to the FA as the England under-21s manager in 2013. It was a key job as the team fed directly into the national team. He had got better and better at it as the youngsters learned his ways and trusted his tactics. In 2016, England Under-21s won the Toulon tournament.

England World Beaters

The "development" plan that Gareth put in place at the FA in 2013 has been hugely successful. England have been unstoppable. After they won the Toulon tournament in 2016 for the under-21 teams they won the next two tournaments. Only France and Brazil have now won more. It is a twelve-team tournament held every year.

MASTERPLAN

The same players that Gareth had coached and made better down the years through his youth work at the FA were now some of England's biggest stars. So Gareth had no worries at all that he could do the senior job.

Not everyone was convinced. The public didn't want a manager so inexperienced and unproven. They wanted one with a fearsome reputation. But that hadn't worked in the past.

Gareth was made caretaker manager, which meant that if he did well, he would get the job . If not, the FA could always say he was only a stop-gap, and look for someone new.

The pressure was huge, though. England were trying to qualify for the 2018 World Cup.

It didn't worry Gareth, and his England team qualified with ease. They were going to the 2018 World Cup finals in Russia! And if that hadn't been enough to convince the FA that Gareth was their man, a 2–2 draw previously in a friendly against the mighty Spain was also key. Gareth got the job as manager and a four-year contract!

This is the clever bit. Gareth turned out to be the best-qualified person for the England job for five reasons:

1. He knew what good young players – and England had a lot of them – needed in order to perform to their best. This didn't mean screaming at them to try harder like Alan Smith. In those frightening moments years before, much of England's brilliant football was born.

2. He knew that a lot of England players were scared when playing for the national team – scared of losing. And when players are afraid, their muscles get tight,

they can't think straight and they make mistakes. So Gareth set about preparing them for every small thing that could happen. And if things go wrong, he told his players: "Don't worry, I'll deal with it."

3. He knew that players were also afraid of the media. If they did make a mistake, the newspapers would be rude about them. So he invited all the football reporters to meet the squad before the World Cup. Just to talk and get to know each other. The players and the reporters saw each other as human beings.

4. He knew how to build team spirit. He took the squad to a Royal Marines training camp in Devon where they left their mobile phones at home, camped under the stars and did lots of challenges like an obstacle course with a tunnel filled with freezing water.

5. He knew that players just want to be happy. So he wrote them letters before the tournament, saying how good he thought they were and that they should relax and trust their natural game. Players' family members were allowed to

come in and visit them at their hotel in Russia.

What did the players do for him in return? They trusted him. They knew him. By the time of the World Cup, ten of his squad had been with him in those under-21 tournaments. Six players – Jordan Pickford, John Stones, Dele Alli, Jesse Lingard, Raheem Sterling and Harry Kane – were in his first eleven.

TAKING ON
THE WORLD

So you see, England always had a great chance in the 2018 World Cup in Russia, even though most people had written them off before they even started. Not many people changed their view after the first match, a nervous 2–1 win against Tunisia. A last-minute Harry Kane goal might have seemed lucky, but it just made the players believe more.

Gareth had told them it might be a long wait for a goal and for the players to remain calm and patient. Their chance would come.

After that, they were flying.

Thrash!

In the next game, they beat Panama 6–1. Now the players really started to believe.

Even a loss to Belgium in their last group game didn't hurt their confidence. Gareth wisely rested several of his best players to keep them fresh for the knockout stage, where Colombia waited.

Penalties Again!

The last-sixteen tie against Colombia was not for the faint-hearted. England were the better side, but they only had a one-goal lead to show for it – Harry Kane's penalty in the fifty-seventh minute.

From there, England were expected to go on to win comfortably. But the longer the game wore on, Colombia came back into it. Jordan Pickford made one of the great saves, somehow turning a thirty yard piledriver around the post with one hand.

And then, with seconds left, Colombia equalized. England didn't clear a corner and Yerry Mina, the giant defender who would go on to play for Everton, headed home.

Heartbreak! England's players slumped to the floor. They thought they'd wasted their big chance.

Gareth sipped from a water bottle. He looked as cool as a cucumber.

The match would be decided on penalties. Gareth wasn't worried. Nor were the England players. Despite the team's dreadful record in penalty shootouts in major competitions (they had won just once), they were confident.

That was down to Gareth. He had prepared them carefully for this moment. Pickford, the goalie, had the names of the Colombia players written on his water bottle and which way they would kick the ball.

And Pickford saved not once, but twice!

It was down to Eric Dier, the Tottenham Hotspur defender, to score the winning penalty. When he did, the England players celebrated wildly. Gareth ran onto the pitch punching the air and shouting over and over again: "Yes!"

He did take time, however, to console the Colombia players who had missed from the spot. He knew how they felt.

COULD THEY WIN IT?

In the quarter-final, England breezed past Sweden, winning 2–0. Harry Maguire scored with a bullet header in the first half and Dele Alli notched another header in the second.

Gareth was on the pitch again, punching the air in front of the England fans. Back home, people really began to think England could win it.

And Gareth was becoming a hero. Southgate tube station in London was temporarily renamed Gareth Southgate station. And his trademark blue waistcoat, that he wore at every game, became the fashion statement that everyone wanted to copy!

Waiting in England's first semi-final in a major tournament since 1990 were Croatia. Everyone thought they were very beatable. Just one more win and England would be in the final!

For the first forty-five minutes, England were in total command. They took a 1–0 lead through a brilliant Kieran Trippier free kick.

Smack!

The Tottenham player curled it beautifully into the corner of the goal after just five minutes.

Harry Kane should have scored another goal, somehow hitting the post from about two yards out! England didn't want the half to end.

But in the second half it was all Croatia, and there was a strange feeling of inevitability about their equalizer.

After ninety minutes and 1–1, the match went into extra time. John Stones had a header cleared off the line. So close! And just when England looked as though they might get to penalties, their defence hesitated for just a millisecond and the Croatia striker scored. England lost 2–1.

Guess what? Gareth was calm about the loss. His team had come so close. But, deep down, he knew they weren't quite ready for a major final. They had to get better.

HISTORY
REPEATS ITSELF

The European Championships of 2020 were delayed for a year because of the coronavirus pandemic. But when summer 2021 rolled round, England were raring to go for glory on home soil.

For Gareth, it was like Euro '96 all over again. The country caught football fever. With every game England played, there was more and more belief that, finally, they would win their first major title since 1966.

Everywhere you went, there were England flags. The football team and Gareth were all people could talk about.

The madness began from England's first game. Who should they face but none other than Croatia? Although they won only 1–0, England were much the better side. Gareth was right, England had got better. They had got their revenge.

Next up came Scotland, and this was where England had a wobble. They were terrible! They barely had a shot on target and were lucky not to lose. They escaped with a 0–0 draw.

Gareth was calm again. While others were getting overexcited or too downcast, he remained level. He refused to get carried away.

In their final group game, England beat the Czech Republic 1–0. They were through to the last sixteen. Up and down the country, England fans were plotting their team's route to the final.

Germany was the first team that stood in their way! Just like Euro '96 again. England's biggest rivals and for fans old enough to remember Euro '96 and the World Cup in 1990, the team who always dashed England's dreams.

Not this time! England were brilliant. They were so calm and professional. They won 2–0 with goals from Raheem Sterling and Harry Kane in the second half. The country went berserk!

Not nearly as much, though as it did when England thrashed Ukraine 4–0 in the quarter-final in Rome!

HEARTBREAK AGAIN

Next up was Denmark in the semi-final. This was a nervous affair, particularly as England conceded a goal and went behind for the first time in the tournament.

Like their manager, the team didn't panic, and they equalized really quickly through Raheem Sterling. England bombarded the Denmark goal but Kasper Schmeichel, the Leicester City goalie, was brilliant. He saved from Harry Maguire. Then Mason Mount. Then Harry Kane.

The match went to extra time. England won a penalty through a brilliant run from Sterling. But guess what? It was saved by Schmeichel.

But England and Gareth didn't even have time to worry that their chance had gone. A millisecond later, England were 2–1 up! The ball rebounded straight back to penalty-taker Kane who scored this time. England were in the final!

Gareth couldn't help but look back to the World Cup semi-final in Moscow. "We've put that right," he said.

Of course we all know what happened next. In the final. England, despite taking the lead in the third minute through Luke Shaw, couldn't get the job done. They lost on penalties. Just like Euro '96, except this time, it was Gareth who was consoling his players who missed.

There is a photo of Terry Venables hugging Gareth all those years ago after his penalty kick was saved. And there is another photo of Gareth hugging Bukayo Saka after his miss. The two images look almost the same.

Typically, Gareth said that the defeat was his fault. "In terms of the penalties, that is my call and totally rests with me."

He was protecting his players again. Being totally

selfless. What a hero!

And whatever happens next for England and Gareth, he can be sure of one thing. He made England serious contenders again, and a lot of people said that wasn't possible.

Of course what happens next is the World Cup, the biggest prize of all. England under Southgate qualified for the tournament, to be held in Qatar in 2022, with ease. They now have a thirty-game unbeaten run in World Cup qualifiers. It is probably their best chance of winning the trophy since the 1990 event when they lost in the semi-finals. Gareth has said that the semi-final defeat to Croatia in Russia and the Euro 2021 final loss to Italy can only help his players learn from big-match experience. As for himself, he signed a new contract to be England manager to the end of 2024. So the England team will be in safe hands for some time yet. And regardless of the on-field action England are now a major force in the world game. For so many years they were either laughed at or underachieved. Gareth changed all of that.

Gareth's Appearances and Goals

Crystal Palace 1988–1995   Appearances 191, goals 22

Aston Villa 1995–2001   Appearances 247, goals 9

Middlesbrough 2001–2006   Appearances 204, goals 4

England   Appearances 57, goals 2

Gareth's Clubs

Crystal Palace

Club name: Crystal Palace
Nickname: The Eagles, Palace
Founded: 1905
Home stadium: Selhurst Park
Current league: Premier League
Current manager: Patrick Vieira
Crest: an eagle holding a ball

Aston Villa

Club name: Aston Villa
Nickname: Villa, The Villans
Founded: 1874
Home stadium: Villa Park
Current league: Premier League
Current manager: Steven Gerrard
Crest: a yellow lion

Middlesbrough

Club name: Middlesbrough
Nickname: Boro
Founded: 1876
Home stadium: The Riverside
Current league: Championship
Current manager: Chris Wilder
Crest: a red lion

Playing Honours

1993–94   Captain Crystal Palace to First Division title

1995–96   Wins League Cup with Aston Villa

1996   European Championships finals with England

1998   World Cup finals for England

2000   Runner-up in FA Cup final. European Championship finals with England

2002   World Cup finals for England

2003–04   Wins League Cup with Middlesbrough

2006   Runner-up in UEFA Cup final with Middlesbrough

Best goals

Crystal Palace v Sheffield United, Premier League 1992

Gareth picked up a loose ball in midfield, jinked forward and then unleashed a fierce right-foot shot into the top left-hand corner of the goal.

Aston Villa v Blackburn 1996

Villa were attacking Blackburn but the defence cleared the ball to the edge of the area. It fell to Gareth. He took one touch and, then, *bang!* A right-foot shot into the top right-hand corner.

Crystal Palace v Blackburn 1992

That 1996 goal was made years earlier. It was almost identical. Apart from this time when the ball came out Gareth didn't take the touch. He hit it first time from twenty yards and it arrowed high into the net.

Did you know?

Gareth is still best friends with Andy Woodman, who he met when they were both in Palace's youth team. Andy had a long career as a professional goalkeeper and his son, Freddie, is a goalie with Newcastle.

In 2019, Gareth received an OBE from Prince Charles at Buckingham Palace for England's semi-final run in the 2018 World Cup. An OBE stands for Officer of the Most Excellent Order of the British Empire.

Gareth married his wife Alison in 1997. They have two children, Mia and Flynn. The family live in Harrogate, Yorkshire.

After his penalty in 1996, Gareth appeared in an advert for Pizza Hut which made fun of his miss. He starred alongside Chris Waddle and Stuart Pearce, former England players who had missed from the spot in the 1990 World Cup semi-final loss to West Germany.